<u>Defend Your Money Against Government Confiscation</u>

*How to Protect Your Savings & Retirement
From the Desperate, Bankrupt Government*

By Damon Geller

What You Will Gain from This Book

- Profit from the Fed's monetary mismanagement
- Steadily grow your investments
- Reduce risk of traditional paper investments
- Significantly outperform the stock market
- Achieve your investment goals

What You Will Learn from This Book

- Learn how gold profits from government collapse
- Learn how your money is vulnerable to confiscation
- Learn the signs when it's time to invest in gold
- Learn how gold hedges against the falling dollar
- Learn about the best investments in gold & silver

Who Else Will Benefit the Most from This Book

- Younger investors building toward their retirement
- Older investors seeking to protect their wealth
- Value investors seeking long-term performance

TABLE OF CONTENTS

Invitation from the Author

After the release of my previous book, "Rescue Your Money from the National Debt Disaster," our desperate government began making controversial moves to access citizen's cash and financial accounts across the globe. Major publications like The Washington Post and New York Times started reporting on unconstitutional government seizures of millions in private citizen wealth. The reason? Because government debt and excess have gone beyond the tipping point, and the folks we've elected to office have turned to our private savings & retirement to keep feeding the machine of government. Thus, I chose to write this book to warn hard-working Americans about the dangers of keeping your savings & retirement in paper assets like cash, stocks and bank accounts, and to give you a proven alternative to protecting your savings & retirement that has outlasted every currency and government for over 5,000 years. Naturally, I cannot address all your questions and concerns in a book, so I invite you to contact us directly with any of your investment questions during or after reading this book. You can call us at 866-925-6626 and you can learn more on our website, www.WholesaleDirectMetals.com.

I welcome the opportunity to assist you.

Damon Geller
President
Wholesale Direct Metals

The 7 Fundamental Reasons to Own Gold

1. Gold has outperformed and outlasted every paper currency ever printed
2. Gold remains the ultimate form of payment with no counterparty risk
3. Gold acts as safe haven in times of rising geopolitical crises
4. Gold has significantly outperformed the stock market since the U.S. came off the gold standard
5. Gold prices rise as national debt rises; gold would need to exceed the $10,000 mark to counterbalance all U.S. public debt held in foreign hands
6. Gold is being bought at a record pace by central banks and governments around the world to hedge against economic collapse
7. Gold outperforms paper assets that are plagued by negative real interest rates

YOUR MONEY IS TARGETED FOR CONFISCATION

Government confiscation of private wealth typically takes the form of inflation or taxation. But in recent years in the United States and across the globe, governments have turned to more nefarious methods of private wealth confiscation in order to maintain their power structure. Throughout America, police are seizing cash from innocent citizens without ever charging them with a crime. Bankers are conspiring with the IRS to seize the accounts of innocent citizens with no notification, no court order, and no charge of crimes. The IMF has proposed global wealth confiscation as a means of funding bankrupt governments. And Congress has passed several controversial laws to make your savings & retirement a prime target for confiscation. To understand how all this happened in a supposedly free society, you need only look back to the events of 2008.

In the fall of 2008, the banking industry collapsed due to years of the most reckless gambling of private money in the history of the world. In order to rescue the Too-Big-To-Fail, Too-Big-To-Jail banks, the U.S. government and the Fed pumped trillions of dollars of YOUR money into the banks and stock market over the next several years. This unprecedented paper money-printing catapulted the U.S. debt to record levels. (Treasury estimates put the debt at $28 trillion by 2018!) But the U.S. government and the Fed ran out of stimulus ammo, with the Fed no longer able to buy U.S. treasuries at the rate needed to prop up the bond market.

So what does a desperate government do to maintain their own power when tax revenues are not enough? In order to keep the Ponzi scheme going, the U.S. government has made several highly controversial moves to make your savings & retirement a prime target for confiscation. And it's becoming clearer by the day, if you want to protect your savings and retirement from government confiscation, your only choice is to keep some of your wealth "outside the system" and in the form of physical gold & silver.

A Starving Government Feeds on Its Citizens

Government officials don't produce anything. They only feed off of those who do. They certainly don't produce wealth; they only redistribute YOUR wealth. And when government officials cannot meet their obligations or fulfill the promises they made to the public, they figure out ways to appropriate the public's money to fund their projects. Desperate government officials will always resort to expropriation, be it through inflation, debt accumulation or deficit.

With the Federal Reserve currently buying 90% of the U.S. Treasury market (and going insolvent doing so), who do you think the government will lean on to pick up the slack? The answer is YOU. In fact, the U.S. government has made several highly controversial moves to make your savings & retirement accounts a prime target for confiscation! They're using legislation and authoritarian power in collusion with the modern financial system to gain access to your private assets in the name of "protection", "security" or "national emergency." But in reality, your savings & wealth are being targeted as a revenue source.

You will soon be forced to use a portion of your savings & retirement to purchase U.S. government debt – debt that will ultimately default, as it is not possible to sustain our astronomical debt nor the deficits that create it. How can they do this? Well, the "beauty" of the modern financial system – to a banker or an insolvent government – is the ease at which they can access your wealth with the stroke of a computer or a new law or tax.

FATCA Gives the IRS Worldwide Power

The government can't put its paws on your money if it doesn't know where it is. And the more information a government has on the movement, location & size of global citizen wealth, the more efficiently and effectively it can create legislation & systems to control that wealth. So the recent FATCA provision requires foreign financial institutions such as banks, stock brokers, hedge funds, pension funds, insurance companies, and trusts to report all U.S. citizens' accounts directly to the IRS. FATCA even requires reporting to the IRS by foreign private companies on any income made by a citizen of the U.S. whether they live here or not. And FATCA will negatively impact the U.S. dollar, the global economy, and our international relationships.

CARDS Gives the Gov't Access to All Brokerage Accounts

The Financial Industry Regulatory Authority, which oversees how investments are sold, proposed what it calls

CARDS – Comprehensive Automated Risk Data System – which is an electronic system that will regularly collect data on balances and transactions in all 4100 brokerages nationwide. CARDS is disguised as a way to "protect" investors, but the system is clearly designed to have detailed information on the structure & location of every citizens' investments. Since the government needs us to support its debt (because outside interests no longer do), wouldn't it be convenient to know and control the structure or every investment portfolio in America?

MyRA: Your Savings Pays for U.S. Debt

In his State Of The Union Address – and coincidentally just as soon as the Fed started tapering their enormous QE treasury-buying experiments – Obama announced the creation of the MyRA. MyRA means your retirement money will now be used to pay for U.S. debt. The MyRA is nothing more than an investment scam being sold to the American people as a you-can't-lose, zero-risk investment by the pitchman-in-chief himself. The reality is, since the Fed can't conjure up money from thin air to buy the debt anymore, and our foreign friends don't want our debt anymore, Obama needs to sell it to John Q. Public. Since the federal government has done so well at everything from delivering mail to affordable healthcare, what could possibly go wrong with jumping into the investment advisory business? Where do I sign up?

Banks Conspire with Gov't to Confiscate Accounts

Think your money is safe in the bank? Think again. A recent bombshell from the New York Times exposed that the nation's biggest banks have willingly turned bank accounts over to the government for total confiscation. It's all done in secrecy, often initiated by the bankers. Tragically, bank account holders don't even know they're being targeted until after the money is seized from their accounts. The banks' deplorable actions have resulted in millions of dollars stolen from U.S. citizens without a shred of due process. And in 80% of the cases, no criminal charges were ever filed. Even more alarming – in a matter of just a few years – these cases of unconstitutional bank account seizures have risen over 500%!

The 4th Amendment of the Constitution reads clearly: "The right of the people to be secure in their persons, houses, papers, and effects against unreasonable searches and seizures, shall not be violated." But according to this shocking New York Times report, the 4th Amendment is under siege.

By law, banks are required to report cash deposits over $10,000 to the IRS. But now, banks are voluntarily – without any requirement from the government – reporting millions of cash deposits under $10,000. From there, the IRS is arbitrarily deeming these deposits suspicious and seizing all the money in these accounts – without any evidence of a crime, without filing criminal charges, and without allowing the account holder to fight the confiscation in court.

As the New York Times reported, the big banks are allowing over 100 multiagency task forces to comb through your bank reports on a daily basis, looking for accounts to seize. Under the Bank Secrecy Act, banks filed more than 700,000 suspicious activity reports last year alone! So do you really think you can trust your local bank?

The number of IRS seizures has increased over 500% in just a few years, and in 80% of the cases the IRS never files a criminal complaint against the individual being seized. The median amount seized by the IRS is $34,000, while legal costs can easily mount to $20,000 or more. Individuals who are the victims of seizure often cannot afford to fight.

How big are the accounts the bankers turn over to the government for seizure? The following are just a few of the horrifying cases exposed by the New York Times:

- The government confiscated $447,000 from a family business in New York

- The government confiscated $33,000 from a small restaurant owner in Iowa

- The government confiscated $66,000 from an army sergeant in Virginia who was saving the money for his daughter's college education

This giant asset forfeiture program gives the government the authority to confiscate your money without due process, even if you've committed no crime! And the bankers are more than happy to aid the government in this outright THEFT. Bankers and the government have gone after run-of-the-mill business owners and wage earners without so much as an allegation that they have committed serious crimes. The government just takes the money without ever filing a criminal complaint, and the owners are left to prove they are innocent. Many give up and never get their money back.

Police Seize Money from Innocent U.S. Citizens

In learning about the massive bank account seizures, you might think your money is safer as cash in your hands. Think again. As revealed in a recent Washington Post report, the executive branch of government has seized money from thousands of innocent U.S. citizens with absolutely no due process. Police departments around the country, at the command of the Justice Department & Homeland Security, have confiscated money from over 200,000 citizens – in some cases tens of thousands of dollars – even though many of them committed no crime! Why? Because our state & federal governments are broke, bankrupt and in desperate need of capital. Just like the administration, law enforcement is shredding the Constitution and rule of law. The Police State is now being expanded to unlawfully gain access to citizens' money.

Unknown to most citizens, police officers around the country received training and financial support from the departments of Homeland Security and Justice to engage in the practice of "highway interdiction" – which involves the police using minor infractions as an excuse to stop citizens, request warrantless searches, and seize cash. In most cases, no crime has been committed and the police never make an arrest.

As part of highway interdiction, the enforcers within the Executive Branch of the U.S. Government – the police – have seized an enormous amount of money from innocent U.S. citizens through a Justice Department program known as "Equitable Sharing." Equitable sharing, the federal government's largest asset forfeiture program, gives the executive branch of government the authority to confiscate your money without due process, even if you've committed no crime!

The Washington Post obtained a database from the Justice Department containing details about 212,000 seizures through the Equitable Sharing Program, likely totaling in the hundreds of millions of dollars or more. The following are just a few of the horrifying cases exposed by the Washington Post:

- Police confiscated $32,000 from a New York man after stopping him because he had a cracked windshield

- Police confiscated $17,550 from a Virginia man after stopping him because his car windows were tinted

- Police confiscated $13,000 from a North Carolina man after stopping him for no offense whatsoever

- Police confiscated $2,400 from a Nevada man after stopping him for no offense whatsoever

Government Confiscation Is Now a Global Trend

Maybe you think you're safe moving your accounts off-shore? Think again. As first reported by Forbes, the International Monetary Fund (IMF) dropped a bomb in its Fiscal Monitor Report. The report paints a dire picture for high-debt nations that fail to aggressively "mobilize domestic revenue," which is code for "aggressively tax its citizens." It goes on to build a case for drastic measures and recommends a series of escalating income and consumption tax increases – culminating in the direct confiscation of assets.

First, here is the excerpt where the IMF clearly advocates a tax on your private savings to pay down government debt:

> "The sharp deterioration of the public finances in many countries has revived interest in a "capital levy"—a one-off tax on private wealth—as an exceptional measure to restore debt sustainability... The tax rates needed to bring down public debt to pre-crisis levels are sizable. Reducing debt ratios to end-2007 levels would require a tax rate of about 10 percent on households with positive net wealth."

You read that right: the IMF wants to take 10% of your private savings in addition to the taxes you're already paying. But is that only the beginning of the proposed wealth confiscation? The report's most chilling aspect is the clinical manner in which it discusses how all governments can work together to track and tax your savings:

> "Financial wealth is mobile, and so, ultimately, are people. ... There may be a case for taxing different forms of wealth differently according to their mobility... Substantial progress likely requires enhanced international cooperation to make it harder for the very well-off to evade taxation by placing funds elsewhere."

As Forbes points out, there are three key points to take away from this report:

1. IMF economists know there are not enough rich people to fund today's governments even if 100 percent of the assets of the 1 percent were expropriated. That means that all households with positive net wealth—everyone with retirement savings or home equity—would have their assets plundered under the IMF's formulation.

2. Such a repudiation of private property will not pay off Western governments' debts or fund budgets going forward. It will merely "restore debt sustainability," allowing free-spending sovereigns to keep tapping the bond markets until the next crisis comes along—for which stronger measures will be required, of course.

3. If politicians should fail to engage in this kind of wholesale robbery, the only alternative scenario the IMF posits is government bankruptcy and

hyperinflation. The IMF makes no proposal to reign in the Ponzi-scheme entitlement programs that are bankrupting us.

Forbes argues that this is where the bankruptcy of the modern entitlement state is taking us—capital controls and exit restrictions "so the proverbial four wolves and a lamb can vote on what's for dinner."

So it's become painfully clear that the United States government and governments across the globe are absolutely desperate to remain solvent and preserve their power structure, to the point of shredding our liberties and constitutional protections in seizing our private assets without due process.

There's Only One Place to Hide

With our desperate governments gaining unprecedented access to your personal savings anywhere in the world, you need to take action NOW to protect your savings & retirement from outright confiscation. But if the government has its hands in your bank accounts, retirement accounts, brokerage accounts, and even the cash in your pocket, is any place safe?

Absolutely. There's ONE asset class this sits outside the financial system and is completely secure from government confiscation and global economic collapse: gold & silver. Gold & silver have been the best wealth protectors for over 5,000 years and have survived every government & currency collapse in history. Today, physical gold & silver sell in record numbers around the globe. Central banks around the world and nations like China are stockpiling gold as a hedge to any possible collapse of all the dollars they hold.

The government has spent way beyond its limits. And now you know that the government is seizing control of your financial accounts. So the time is now. Protect your savings & retirement with physical gold & silver before you have nothing left to protect.

GET READY FOR $3000 GOLD

In the previous chapter, we revealed how the government confiscates paper wealth in all its forms. Next, we're going to examine all the conditions that led our nation to the brink of collapse, starting with the national debt disaster. The broken political and criminal banking systems we have today are reliant on endless debt accumulation for their survival. So to enable politicians and bankers to carry out their will, the Federal Reserve prints money at a breakneck pace with zero accountability to the American taxpayer. Meanwhile, the president – whether red or blue – has done nothing to stop it. Why? Because the Fed chief is the most powerful human on earth, period. And he or she does not answer to either side of the political aisle. The tragic result of this massive Federal Reserve money-printing has been a systematic destruction of wealth and an enormous rise in REAL inflation. What's more, not only has the Fed doomed your paper-based savings and retirement, but the Fed's actions have guaranteed $3000 gold.

Politicians & Bankers: An Unholy Marriage

When it comes to money, there is no democracy or freedom, and there are no nations or citizens. Money is ruled by a plutocracy of financial institutions. They make the laws, they rule the world, and they move or remove anyone that doesn't promote or support their agenda. And in order for them to survive and achieve "growth," they rely on the constant accumulation of new public DEBT. In a monetary system where every dollar is created from debt, the system becomes a Ponzi scheme and only works until it collapses. This is illustrated throughout history, as every civilization and every paper currency has imploded under huge debt loads and a systemic lack of solvency.

Debt Has Doomed the Nation & the Dollar

In January of 2001, the national debt stood at $5.7 trillion. By January of 2009, the national debt had ballooned to around $11 trillion – a doubling of U.S. debt in 8 years! Obama came into office in 2009 promising hope and change. But did he really change anything in terms of our debilitating national debt? Absolutely not. At the command of the Federal Reserve, our national debt will skyrocket to around $25 trillion by the time Obama leaves office. In short, the Fed will have increased the national debt 5 times in the span of two presidencies. The chart below shows the dramatic rise in U.S. debt since 2001:

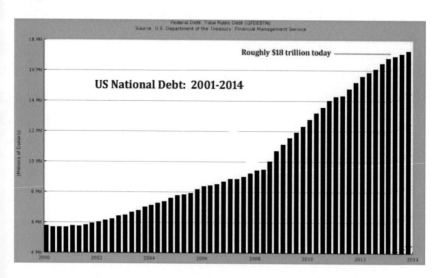

Everyone knows you can't stockpile $25 trillion in debt without serious consequences. What serious consequences? The chart below shows the alarming loss in value of the U.S. dollar versus other currencies since 2001:

As you can see, the U.S. Dollar lost 33% of its value versus other currencies since 2001!

Debt Has Skyrocketed Gas & Gold

As the Federal Reserve drove up debt to record numbers, what happened to gold? The chart below shows the tremendous increase in gold's value since 2001:

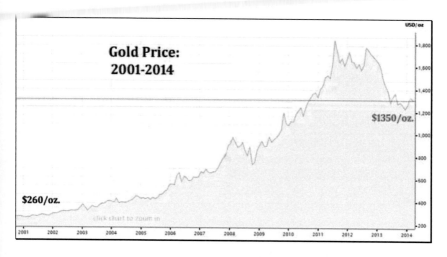

As you can see, gold increased over 5 TIMES in value since 2001! And this is including gold's correction in 2013. So not only has gold increased 5 times since 2001, it's once again a great value at these levels.

Where Are We Headed?

The U.S. Treasury tells us that the U.S. debt will reach $28 trillion by 2018, regardless of who the next president is. That's a staggering 58% increase in U.S. debt from where we are today. Why will this happen? Because neither party has shown any serious commitment whatsoever to reduce government spending. And this will only result in further destruction of the U.S. dollar until the dollar finally collapses and ceases to be the world's reserve currency, just as ALL global currencies have failed throughout history.

And based upon Treasury's debt projections, here is where gold is going:

2015 U.S. Debt = 21T | Gold = $1,640/oz.
2016 U.S. Debt = 22.7T | Gold = $2,120/oz.
2017 U.S. Debt = 25.5T | Gold = $2,560/oz.
2018 U.S. Debt = 28T | Gold = $3,000/oz.

As the Fed rockets us to $28 trillion in debt, these projections put gold at $3000/oz. by 2018!

Protect Yourself Now before the Next Collapse

It is a catastrophe that one person, like Janet Yellen or Ben Bernanke, can control the price of everything. But that's the centrally-planned world we live in, and that is precisely why your wealth doesn't and shouldn't care who wins in 2016 or beyond. According to the Fed and the U.S. Treasury, debt will explode in the next decade or until the Ponzi scheme collapses. As a result, the economic system will crash, the dollar will lose its global reserve status, and gold will soar.

So when it comes to your money, you need to fight the forces bankrupting our nation and destroying the value of your savings & wealth. How do you protect yourself? The answer is obvious: gold & silver. As the charts above clearly demonstrate, gold & silver track U.S. debt more than any other asset on earth. So as the debt nearly doubles again to $28 trillion by 2018, where do you think your money needs to be?

THE DEATH OF THE U.S. DOLLAR

For the last 600 years, there have been six different global reserve currencies controlled by world superpowers. The latest – the U.S. dollar – has dominated world currency for over 80 years. The alarming fact is, global reserve currencies have collapsed every 80-90 years for the last six centuries! What does this mean for America and the dominance of the U.S. dollar? Based on recent evidence and long-standing historical trends, experts predict the imminent collapse of the U.S. dollar! What's more alarming? Many Americans aren't yet doing the one thing that will save their savings & retirement from U.S. dollar collapse.

The Crisis Generation

600 years of human history has shown that the average lifespan of a global reserve currency is equal to a "saeculum" – or "human lifetime" – of about 80-90 years, broken down into four 20-year generations. The best-selling book, "The Fourth Turning," goes through history and demonstrates this 4-phase evolution:

First generation: High

This is an era when institutions are strong and society is confident about where it wants to go. America's most recent First Turning was the post-World War II American High, beginning in 1946 and ending with the assassination of President John F. Kennedy.

Second generation: Awakening

This is an era when institutions are attacked in the name of personal and spiritual autonomy. People suddenly tire of social discipline and want to recapture a sense of personal authenticity. America's most recent Awakening was the "Consciousness Revolution," which spanned from the campus and inner-city revolts of the mid-1960s to the reelection of Ronald Reagan.

Third generation: Unraveling

This is an era when institutions are weak and distrusted, while individualism is strong and flourishing. America's most recent Unraveling was the Long Boom and Culture War, beginning in the mid-1980s and ending in the late 2000s.

Fourth generation: Crisis

This is an era in which institutional life is destroyed and rebuilt in response to a perceived threat to the nation's survival. America's most recent Fourth Turning began with the stock market crash of 1929 and climaxed with the end of World War II.

America is now in this fourth "crisis" phase, about 80-90 years from the beginning of the first phase. It is in this "fourth turning" crisis that institutional life will be torn down and rebuilt from the ground up. This rebuilding is always in response to a perceived threat to the nation's very survival. Is there any question that right now our nation's very survival is at risk? Based on history, we are right smack in the crisis period, and full breakdown of all our current "systems" are scheduled to happen sometime between now and 2020. This systemic breakdown means there will be major changes in the world's financial system and reserve currency.

Want proof? Just take a look at the graph below. It shows the lifespan of dominant currencies going back 600 years. Notice that the U.S. dollar has now been the dominant currency for 88 years, about the same length of time as its predecessors:

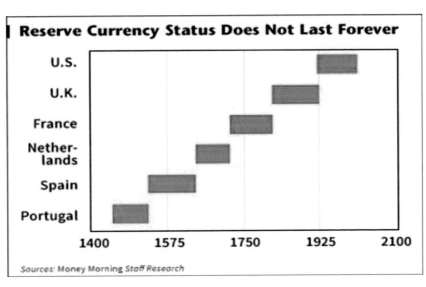

So when you combine the lifespan of dominant currencies throughout history with the fact that we're entering the "Crisis" generation, it's obvious why experts say that the U.S. dollar's days as the world's reserve currency are coming to a climactic end.

All Fiat Currencies Collapse

"Fiat" currency is paper currency backed by nothing tangible. As opposed to "sound money" which is was backed by gold or some other valuable commodity, a fiat currency is backed by nothing more than faith in the government. The U.S. dollar has been a fiat currency since Nixon closed the gold window in 1971 in what was the greatest heist in American history. The scary fact is, the average life span of a fiat currency is 40 years, and the U.S. dollar has now exceeded 40 years as a fiat currency!

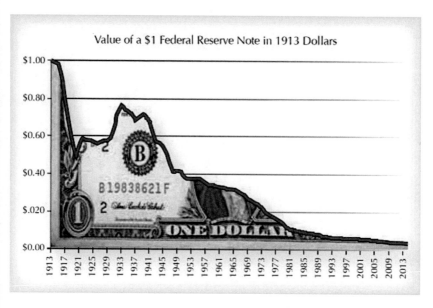

Value of a $1 Federal Reserve Note in 1913 Dollars

Prior to 1933 and for well over 100 years, the dollar was backed by gold, and $20 bought you an ounce of gold. But after the government stole all U.S. citizens' gold in 1933 for a $20 paper certificate, gold was revalued at $35

31

U.S.D., meaning the dollar was devalued by 43% overnight and all foreign and domestic holders of dollars were effectively robbed.

After Nixon closed the gold window completely in 1971, it took $67 to buy an ounce of gold, devaluing the U.S. dollar by 50% again. Today, it takes well over a thousand U.S. dollars to buy that same ounce of gold. Why? Because the U.S. dollar is now nothing more than a fast-declining Federal Reserve note backed by a corrupt government that is saddled with $18 trillion in unpayable debt.

Americans Are Living in Denial

Most everyone reading this was born into U.S. dollar supremacy. So it should come as no surprise that most of America is asleep when it comes to the dollar's coming doom. Unfortunately, that means that there aren't a whole lot of Americans preparing for dollar collapse either. Most folks have been brainwashed by Wall Street and the bank-run mainstream-media to believe in what amounts to nothing more than a grand illusion based on lies...

> *The bankers and their politician puppets have your best interest at heart.*

> *The U.S. dollar will always be king.*

> *Your wealth is safe in a bank.*

> *The financial "system" and stocks are safe (even at ridiculous valuations).*

The economy is actually recovering.

The job market is improving.

Inflation doesn't exist.

People must believe this illusion, because if people actually thought critically about these massive and inevitable shifts in power and wealth preservation, there would be even more Americans buying real gold. There would be far less wealth sitting in the corrupt, criminal and insolvent too-big-to-fail banking system. And the Fed, who monetizes a trillion dollars a year with their criminal QE policies, would be shut down. People would insist that our elected officials start working for the people who elected them, instead of banks and corporations, or they'd throw them out.

But instead, most people are sleepwalking through life believing the perpetual propaganda and lies that they have been told for so long that the illusion has become masked by false hope.

Protect Yourself Before It's Too Late

This paper money experiment has run its course. The Federal Reserve, the U.S. government, and Wall Street crooks have misused their power by mismanaging the dollar, and there will be global repercussions. The debt load sitting on top of the U.S. dollar is unsustainable and will continue to crush the dollar's purchasing power until no one wants to hold U.S. dollars, and they are no longer accepted for global trade. The dollar's collapse means that every single one of your paper investments that are dollar-backed – stocks, mutual funds, money markets, cash accounts, etc. – will go down right along with the dollar! Meanwhile, the government and the banks will find a way to protect themselves at your expense.

So as we say goodbye to the U.S. dollar's dominance, it doesn't have to mean goodbye to your savings & retirement. Remove at least some of your savings & retirement from the dollar-backed, paper-based financial system and protect it with the one asset that has outlasted every fiat currency ever invented for the last 5,000 years: Gold.

REAL INFLATION IS 5 TIMES WHAT THE GOV'T CLAIMS

Inflation is as violent as a mugger, as frightening as an armed robber and as deadly as a hit man.

— Ronald Reagan

The U.S. dollar's rapid collapse means your purchasing power has collapsed too. But don't tell that to the government! Right now, the administration, the Federal Reserve, and the bank-controlled mainstream media continue to claim that inflation is low and completely under control, despite the fact that the prices of things we really need are rising at a breakneck pace. Don't be fooled: REAL inflation is killing this country, regardless of the lies we're being told. Whether food, housing, or education, we're all choking on runaway inflation that is actually 5 times what the government claims! So as the lies about inflation persist, we are actually stuck in a spiral of runaway inflation that will cripple the U.S. economy and destroy your savings & retirement. And not even the record-setting stock market can protect you from its wrath.

Government Inflation Data Is a Lie

At a recent Fed meeting, Janet Yellen told the mainstream media how inflation is just "noise" and that it's fine and coming in line with the Fed's 2% target. Hopefully you can eat "noise," because you certainly can't use it to buy food. Of course, you know that the government's claims of 2% inflation is a bunch of hogwash if you eat food, heat your home, drive a car, go to a doctor, educate your kids, or pay for housing.

The lie begins with the way the inflation rate is calculated. Since the 1970s, the government has manipulated its official formula for inflation more than 20 times, and at this point it bears so little relation to reality that it is essentially meaningless. Dr. Paul Craig Roberts, one of the voices of reason who worked at Treasury under Reagan, put this in a historical perspective:

"During the Clinton regime, the Boskin Commission rigged the inflation measure in order to cheat Social Security recipients out of their cost-of-living adjustments. Anyone who purchases food, fuel, or anything knows that inflation is much higher than the officially reported number."

So we have to ask, do these criminals do their own food shopping? Do they fill up their own gas tanks? Heat their homes? How foolish do they think we are? And how long do they think they can keep this rigged money-printing Ponzi scheme going before REAL inflation becomes hyper-inflation and completely guts our standard of living and destroys our economy?

The REAL Inflation Numbers Are Scary

By stripping away all the bank-controlled government propaganda and lies, and simply looking at real numbers and real data, the reality of inflation becomes crystal clear. In the graph below that covers the last 14 years, you see that while the government's consumer price index (CPI) only rose 39% and the Fed's preferred measure of inflation only rose 32%, the real data behind the rising cost of goods & services tells a much different story. Crude oil rose 314%, a dozen eggs rose 106%, college tuition rose 68%, housing rose 50%, and so on. But Janet Yellen doesn't want you to worry, because that's just "noise."

Living Expense	Jan 2000	March 2014	% Increase
Barrel Of Oil	$24.11	$100	314.80%
Fuel Oil (Per Gallon)	$1.19	$4.07	242.00%
Gallon of Gas	$1.27	$3.51	176.40%
One Dozen Eggs	$0.97	$2.00	106.20%
Annual Healthcare Spending (Per Capita)	$4,550	$9,300	104.40%
Ground Beef (Per lb)	$1.90	$3.73	96.30%
Movie Ticket	$5.25	$10.25	95.20%
Average Private College Tuition	$22,000	$37,000	68.20%
Electricity (Per Kwh)	$0.08	$0.13	59.50%
New Car	$20,300	$31,500	55.20%
Coffee (Per lb)	$3.40	$5.20	52.90%
Natural Gas (Per Therm)	$0.71	$1.08	51.40%
Avg. Home Price (Case Shiller)	$161,000	$242,000	50.30%
Postage Stamp	$0.33	$0.49	48.50%
Avg Monthly Rent (Case Shiller)	$635	$890	40.20%
CPI	$168.80	$234.78	39.09%
PCE Deflator (Fed's Preferred Measure)	$81.78	$107.66	31.65%
Source: David Stockman			

The reality of this chart is clear: If inflation were calculated the same way it was back when Reagan took office, the REAL inflation rate today is actually 10% per year -- 5 times what the government claims! So, why is the government lying about inflation? Because inflation is an insidious tool used by governments and bankers to essentially steal wealth from their citizens, manipulate interest rates, falsify GDP, and create a false sense of security. Inflation has been around for as long as the dollar has been decoupled from gold, and it has only gone in one direction – UP!

How REAL Inflation Boosts Gold & Silver

The best way to judge the effects of REAL inflation is to examine the price of REAL physical assets like gold & silver. In 1913, when the Fed was created, a $20 bill and a $20 gold piece were of EQUAL VALUE. Today, that same $20 paper bill is worth a paltry 85 cents, and that same $20 gold piece is worth over $1400! In 1964, a new car sold for $2000. If you bought $2000 in gold in 1964, it is worth over $75,000 today! And if you bought $2000 in silver in 1964, it is worth over $45,000 today! This means that the same $2000 in precious metals still buys you a nice new luxury car, while $2000 saved in greenbacks will barely buy you an old broken-down jalopy.

Just since 2000, gold rose 400% and silver rose 500%. And since 2008, when Obama took office and the Fed put the printing presses on full speed ahead, food prices have risen 50% and gas prices have risen 70%. But gold & silver have DOUBLED! Which means that by storing wealth in precious metals like gold and silver -- the oldest form of real money -- your purchasing power exceeds real inflation, providing you a significant savings windfall.

Can't the Stock Market Protect Me?

With the stock market hitting new highs just a few years after the global financial collapse, many people think the stock market is the best place to protect their savings & retirement from runaway inflation. Tragically, nothing can be further from the truth. Even with the stock market achieving record highs, the DOW has only increased a paltry 2% per year since 2000. Just look at how that compares to inflation and gold:

Since 2000:

DOW: Up 2% per year

REAL Inflation: Up 10% per year

Gold: Up 13% per year!

So even with the DOW's record gains, you LOST a significant portion of your savings & retirement since 2000 because of runaway inflation. In other words, your small annual stock gains were trumped by the REAL cost increase of goods & services. Meanwhile, gold outpaced REAL inflation by a significant margin, meaning any savings & retirement you kept in gold survived REAL inflation and even earned you significant profit!

The BEST Way to Protect Yourself from REAL Inflation

So as the government continues to destroy the value of your dollars and inflate every cost that is essential to you, gold continues to be the greatest protector against unbacked paper currencies and an excellent hedge against runaway inflation. Gold and silver have outlasted every paper fiat currency every invented by governments and central banks throughout history, and they've outperformed every single other asset class on earth since 2000. Gold and silver also offer significant advantages in the form of privacy, liquidity and security that the modern financial system cannot.

Considering gold and silver's historic track record and their proven ability to protect you from runaway inflation, you can't afford to wait another minute to diversify a portion of your savings out of dollars, out of the bank, and into real physical gold and silver.

FINANCIAL WMDS WILL TAKE DOWN THE WORLD ECONOMY

Everyone knows that the 2008 Global Economic Collapse was caused primarily by banks' unregulated casino-style gambling. Instead of blackjack and slots, the banks bet massively on financial derivatives known as a "credit default swaps," which Warren Buffett famously called "weapons of financial mass destruction." But what most people don't know is that the criminal banks are ignoring Buffet's warning and once again betting massively on swaps, to the tune of over $30 TRILLION – 8 times the budget of the United States Government and more than the entire value of the U.S. stock market! Now that the banks have reopened the casino doors, experts predict that these financial WMDs will take down the global economy worse than we've ever seen.

Big Banks Gamble with YOUR Money

Credit default swaps were invented by banking conglomerate JP Morgan in 1994. Simply put, a credit default swap is an unregulated type of insurance policy against loans going bad. So as banks wrote millions of dangerous loans during the housing bubble, they made an unbelievable fortune selling insurance policies – swaps – on those loans.

But there's one HUGE problem: When you sell insurance policies, you better hope that most buyers don't need to collect on them. It's just like earthquake insurance: as long as there's no earthquake, insurance companies make a fortune on earthquake insurance. But as soon as there's a massive earthquake, insurance companies suddenly go out of business and homeowners are left holding the bag.

This is exactly why Warren Buffet called swaps financial WMDs – because they are as destructive as an atomic bomb.

And here's what happened: When the housing bubble burst and millions of loans went bad, banks were suddenly on the hook to pay the swap-buyers hundreds of billions of dollars. And just like earthquake insurers, they didn't have the money to pay them.

What's worse, other financial institutions had all kinds of counterparty arrangements with these massive banks, so the whole entire system fell like a house of cards. And you, the American taxpayer, spent trillions of dollars to bail out the "Too Big to Fail" criminal banks. But not before the entire global economy collapsed during the 2008 crisis, costing average Americans trillions in their investments and retirement accounts.

History Is About to Repeat Itself – Only Worse

The scary truth is, nothing has changed. In fact, things are now MUCH worse than in 2008, despite Buffett's warning. After YOU bailed out the banks and not a single banker was put in jail, the banks turned around and reopened the casino doors. Today, the largely unregulated credit default swap market is now a staggering $30 TRILLION and growing! How much is $30 trillion? Take a look:

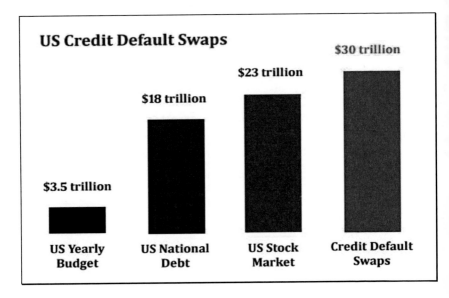

So what happens THIS TIME when $30 trillion in financial weapons of mass destruction blow up in the bankers' faces? Well, one thing is for sure: Governments and central banks no longer have the bankroll to bail out the banks! So that only means one thing... Total collapse of the global banking system!

If you thought a 20-30% dip in your portfolio was bad after 2008, try an 80% collapse when the banking system completely falls apart! Or, the entire financial and banking system comes down like a house of cards. Total meltdown. And this time, The Fed and the U.S. Government won't be there to prop up the stock market and recoup your gains after just a few years. THIS collapse could be deeper and longer-lasting than any we've seen before — even worse than the Great Depression!

Protect Yourself Now, Before It's Too Late

Don't fool yourself into believing you're protected just because you are not personally invested in the financial weapons of mass destruction. Just like in 2008, when the giant banks and other financial institutions collapse due to bad bets on credit default swaps, ANYONE invested in bank-issued paper investments will be taken down with the banks. This includes everyone from national governments to large institutions to average savers & investors.

So, how do you protect yourself when the entire system collapses? The answer... Do what Buffett did. Put a percentage of your savings, retirement & wealth in gold & silver – the #1 asset class that sits OUTSIDE of the financial system and in fact GROWS when paper assets fail. And gold & silver have ZERO exposure to the credit default swap market. When Buffett saw the markets on the verge of collapse, he bought 4,000 tons of silver, weighing more than TEN Boeing 747s! Why? Because gold & silver have survived every fiat currency and every economy the world's ever known and have been the wealth protector of choice for over 5,000 years.

As evidenced in the following chart, gold DOUBLED in the years after the financial collapse of 2008, while Silver increased over 5 times during the same period!

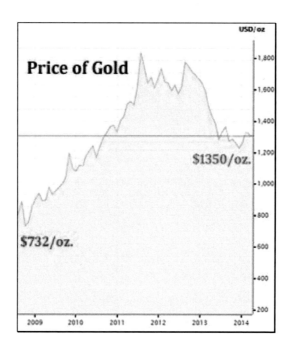

So remind yourself what it was like when Lehman Brothers and Bear Stearns collapsed and your entire portfolio took a nosedive after 2008. Are you willing to go through that and worse, knowing that the U.S. Government and The Fed no longer have enough money-printing ability to once again bail out the financial markets and prop up the stock market? Can you really endure an 80% loss of your savings, retirement or wealth? Wouldn't you rather do what Warren Buffett did and GROW your wealth while everyone else loses theirs? Then get into gold & silver. NOW. Before it's too late for you and your children.

WHY GOLD IS THE ENEMY OF CORRUPT BANKS

One of the questions we commonly get from clients is, "How do I really protect my money in volatile times like these?" Well, it's a good thing you're asking us and not a run-of-the-mill investment adviser or banker. Pose this question to several investment advisers and you'll probably get a different canned answer from each of them. One concept you will hear thrown around is that "diversification" is very important to wealth preservation. I completely agree. Unfortunately, it seems no one really understands true diversification.

In today's times, diversification means that everything you buy from a bank or bank investment house involves a stock, ETF, bond, annuity, CD, etc. The problem is, all of these instruments reside "inside the system." But for true diversification, and to be prepared for the perilous risk facing the current financial system, you need some wealth "outside the system" – outside the fiat currency and paper-based/digital banking system. This way, if "the system" fails, you don't.

The big – or should I say "too big to fail" – banks all use very general risk models and fancy words like "asset allocation" to help decide where to place your money based on your "risk profile," which is seemingly determined by a number of factors including your age, income (if you're still working) and your goals for the future. In reality, the "TBTF" banks don't care where your money goes in terms of different investment vehicles, just as long as it lives with their bank for as long as possible. The more locked up it is, the better.

This is a very important concept to understand, because fractional banking relies on it and it creates imaginary liquidity for the bank. The banker, or "investment advisor" as they may be called, may suggest a municipal bond, a mutual fund, a CD, an individual stock, U.S. treasuries, a combination of all of those things or an Exchange Traded Fund or ETF. For example, just ask an advisor about gold and they'll sell you the ETF "GLD" as fast as they can to keep your money there – and that itself is a disaster waiting to happen.

In the end, the only thing that matters to your banker is that your money, as much as possible, lives with that bank so that the bank can now create even more money from thin air by fractionalizing your wealth and taking risks with your money. Bottom line: if your money is in any traditional paper-based investment or exists simply in the computer of a bank or investment banking company, ALL of your wealth is at risk to a single catastrophic event.

As economist and investment adviser John Mauldin notes, "One of the very real problems we face is the growing feeling that the system is rigged against regular people in favor of "the bankers" or the 1%. And if we are honest with ourselves, we have to admit there is reason for that feeling. Things like LIBOR are structured with a very real potential for manipulation. When the facts come out, there is just one more reason not to trust the system. And if there is no trust, there is no system."

The point of this is not to contrast each different investment-vehicle against the others. It is to make the point that ALL assets outside of hard tangible investment assets live with a bank and can vanish right alongside the banks' capital. In other words, if for example the global financial system were to collapse because of, say, the meltdown of financial WMDs, you could have zero access to any wealth – literally overnight. Look, I have no idea whether the S&P 500 will perform better or worse than a tax-free municipal bond at 5% and, quite frankly, I can't tell you which one has less risk. Your banker, by contrast, would like you to believe the muni is safer, but here's the reality: major cities in California filed for bankruptcy after the most recent banking meltdown.

Therefore, today I wouldn't consider any debt asset completely "safe." Is an annuity right for you? Again, who knows? But they make great sense for the bank, because as soon as you sign on the dotted line, they know your money is not going anywhere for a while and it isn't going to cost them very much to use it. Same situation with a CD. However, what I can tell you is that if you have ALL your wealth with BofA or Charles Schwab and the whole house of cards comes down, it isn't going to matter what fund they have you in.

Let's please be very clear: the bank is not your friend. If you haven't been convinced by the bailouts of 2008, or the interest rates since then, or the banks' unwillingness to make loans to small businesses over the past several years, then you should be convinced by stunning crimes committed by the world's biggest banks. After the MF

Global scandal, the PFG futures-broker scandal and the Libor rate-rigging criminal fraud, how can anyone have all of their wealth sitting in the absolutely corrupt financial and banking system? But then you must remember, perception control is the banker weapon du jour. "When it comes to building wealth, muddying the difference between perception and reality is the key manipulation tool that banksters use to goad people into wrong choices."

So, how do you properly diversify and protect your wealth and retirement? Gold and silver make the most sense as true diversification for many reasons. The simplest reason: they are hard money. We are struggling through a period of severe structural pressure on our global fiat currency systems, and the best hedge to any chaos in them is gold and silver. Gold has outlasted every paper currency ever printed, because all paper currencies throughout history have failed in time. The euro will fail. The dollar will fail. That question has been answered by history. The bigger questions are: what will the new currency look like? Will there be more consolidation or less? Will it be global or regional? How much wealth destruction will occur in the process and – most importantly, how much will gold cost in the new currency?

While no one knows the exact answers to those questions, what we do know from history is that at some point in the near future, there will be a reset of currency and even the very notion of what "money" is, just as there have been many times throughout history. The question is not if, but when. And when the banking system is teetering on collapse and the whole system needs a reset more than it needs another worthless stimulus package, gold is by far the best true diversifier and the only asset of last resort.

THE 7 DEADLY MYTHS OF GOLD INVESTING

Why do I call the fallacious beliefs that prevent people from investing in gold "The 7 Deadly Myths of Gold Investing"? Because quite honestly – as we tell our Wholesale Direct Metals clients – failing to balance your investment portfolio with gold and/or silver can literally be deadly to your savings and investments. Yet sadly, many of the concerns people have about gold are simply based on myths. And once you learn the truth about gold, you'll realize why gold is absolutely fundamental to your overall investment strategy. So let's examine the 7 deadly myths of gold investing.

Deadly Myth #1: The Gold Boom is Over

You're no doubt aware of gold's tremendous performance over the last several years, and maybe you're a little nervous that it might be too late to get in on the gold boom. As a longtime gold dealer at Wholesale Direct Metals as well as an experienced gold investor, I am often asked about gold's price action. These days the questions tend to have a bubble-ish tone to them. The "gold is in a bubble" debates are the easiest one's to counter, albeit the most frustrating.

When someone asks me about gold prices being in a "bubble" or gold's price action resembling the tech stock market of the late 90s or the real estate pandemonium of 2007, they're forgetting a crucial fact about bubbles: For a true investment "bubble" to exist, you need penetration and participation on a massive scale. In the late 90s right before the NASDAQ blew up, everyone owned tech stocks. Tech stocks made up a large portion of people's investment portfolios, and penetration and participation in them was deep and aggressive. Look also at the real estate bubble. Participation was so deep and combined with so much leverage, that in order to melt down, the market didn't even need to fall; it simply needed to stop rising as fast. Lenders would loan money to anyone with a pulse.

By contrast, ask your friends how many of them have bought even a single ounce of real investment gold, let alone a significant portion of their savings or investment capital in real gold or even gold stocks. I can already tell you the answer: not much, if any. Gold makes up 1 to 1.5% of the average American's portfolio today. It's even less of a percentage in 401Ks, IRAs, pensions and other retirement accounts. Yet because of gold's price, people want to talk bubble? Forget the price. The fundamentals that caused gold to double over a three-year period are not only still in place, they are accelerating. Debt, money printing, political indifference, global slowdown, lack of fiscal faith in policy makers, and global uncertainty all mean that now is still a great time to invest in gold.

The concern over gold being in a bubble also says something about the perception of today's fiat currency, the U.S. debt and other forms of paper or "debt-based" savings. Or it simply illustrates the very common lack of understanding in monetary policy or, and even more importantly, the history of money. People who worry that gold is in a bubble are typically comparing what gold is worth in terms of paper money. Their perception is that green paper is a viable benchmark for the cost of goods or assets to be priced in, and they couldn't be more wrong.

By contrast, the central banks that control the world banking system use gold as their store of value and backing to their currencies, because gold has a real value that cannot be debased by monetary policy the way paper money can. Simply put, the more your paper gets diluted, the more your purchasing power is eroded, and the more you need to switch your faith out of paper money and into gold. I try my best to help my clients understand that there is an end-game to debt-based savings and living beyond our means in a debt-based economy. Gold's upward limit can really only be calculated in terms of fiat currencies' downside limit. Yet if a currency's downside limit is zero, think how high can gold go, considering it has outlasted every fiat currency ever made? It's clear that gold will keep rising as long as debt accumulation persists and fiat currencies continue to be debased.

Deadly Myth #2: Gold Is Too Risky of an Investment

We all worry about risky investments. Yet gold and silver often get lumped together erroneously with other paper-based "investments" in the risk basket. I would argue that they should not be, especially gold. As I tell my clients, gold is one of the least risky places you can store your wealth, and it has also been one of the least risky places to find yield. Investments that work are ones that go up and have intrinsic value. Dollars in the bank or government bonds are nothing more than debt-based savings, while gold is real savings. When you consider what the bank is paying, real negative interest rates, and current Fed policy, sitting with your money in a bank has proven to be much riskier than gold.

In addition, looking for wealth preservation or yield in the equities market certainly must be considered risky given its volatility and downswings, not to mention possible failure. When I hear people say they perceive hard gold ownership as "risky," I can't help but hope that they are capable of a change of perspective, because it's their faith in paper that should be seen as risky and is misguided in our professional opinion. When paper provides no return, loses value, loses people's faith, and is intrinsically worth zero, hard monetary-based assets like gold and silver are the least risky assets.

Deadly Myth #3: I Can Get Better Performance from Other Investments

It may very well be possible that you can think of an investment that has done better or "might" do better in the future, but with how much risk? Remember, we're not here to hit home runs for people based on performance. Gold is not a purchase you make to get rich quick. Rather, it's an asset you hold so that you don't get poor quick. Its purpose is to protect against the kind of wealth destruction we saw in 2008 and have seen for 10 years while we've run massive deficits. Gold's main purpose is to act as a wealth preserver and wealth protector. That said, gold has "performed" quite well also. 20% yearly growth on average for the first 11 years of this century is what I would call stellar performance.

Gold's gains are largely due to the effect of the printing of fiat paper and accumulation of debt. It's the indicator and yard-stick against which the debasement of fake (printed) money is valued against. If you're looking for "performance," you should look for it elsewhere in your portfolio, and remember that "performance" equals added risk by default. You buy gold to hedge the items of perceived performance in your portfolio, but don't be surprised if gold continues to outperform most everything else if we keep printing currency, accumulating debt, and spending money we don't have.

Deadly Myth #4: I'm Too Old to Buy Gold

We have a number of clients at Wholesale Direct Metals who are retired and elderly. As they get older, naturally they become more cautious about their investments, and that's a good thing. Yet none of us would ever say, "I'm too old to protect my wealth," or "I'm too old to grow my wealth," or "I'm too old to take a defensive position and hedge the collapsing monetary world around me and protect myself from the madmen trying to centrally plan the global economy, and failing!" Okay, the last one might be a little dramatic, but the concept that, once you're old your money belongs in a bank, is a very dangerous one. I would argue that with negative real interest rates (banks paying a lower interest rate than inflation), it is even more important for a retiree or someone on a fixed income to have a hedge against dollar debasement and inflation. The older you get (and no longer work), the more important safe yield becomes.

Once you become too old to work anymore, you have to look at the longevity of your wealth and invest it in such a way that it lasts longer than you. If or when all this money printing becomes real inflation and your expenses go up but your income doesn't, you better have your savings in a safe place where it can get yield. If expenses are rising – energy costs, water, food, gas, etc. – gold will rise too by its very nature as a dollar-denominated hard asset. So owning gold is even more important as you get into your "golden years."

Deadly Myth #5: Bullion is the Best Way to Invest in Gold

If you watch any cable television these days, you've no doubt seen one gold advertisement after another. And all of them recommend buying gold bullion as the way to enter the gold market. Not surprisingly, a huge percentage of our clients at Wholesale Direct Metals call us initially looking to buy gold or silver bullion. It's at that point we tell them, yes, we'd be more than happy to sell them bullion, "but are you aware of the other gold and silver investment products that offer many advantages over bullion?" Most of the time they are not aware, so we take the opportunity to do what we enjoy most: arm our clients with game-changing investment guidance.

The fact is, bullion is not the only way you can invest in gold and silver, and it's very often not the best way to invest in gold and silver. You can often get the best out of gold and silver by investing in private coins, sometimes referred to as investment-grade coins.

It's a good idea to understand private coin investing before making a major investment in private coins. The good news is, it really just comes down to a simple definition of each. "Bullion" refers to gold that trades solely for its weight, and "private" refers to a coin that has a value premium in addition to its weight, usually because it is limited in population and has some privacy advantages. Bullion can be a bullion coin like a Canadian Maple Leaf or it can be a bar or ingot in various sizes. Bullion is worth nothing more than its weight when selling and, when buying, will be its weight plus a mintage fee. Mintage fees are larger on coins and fractional coins than larger bars, but all bullion has a mintage fee to buy it.

Private coins, by contrast, maintain a premium to their weight and can be sold for their weight plus whatever the current premium is. Private coins also tend to be more stable than bullion as they do not have a paper-traded component. While gold bullion has had an impressive record of profitability since the early 1970's, there really is no comparison with private gold coins. A $10,000 basket of private gold coins in 1970 was worth a stunning $630,000 by 2014, while bullion was only worth $370,000! (see graph on the next page)

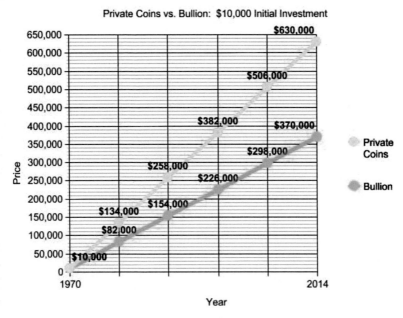

Source: PCGS 3000 Private Coin Index

Private coins also offer more privacy than bullion as they are non-reportable and less visible to the government. With some forms of gold bullion, a 1099 form must be completed. This is not the case for private gold coins, for which there are no reporting requirements whatsoever. Private gold coins are one of the few remaining investments today that can be accumulated privately and confidentially. They are the least visible form of wealth. By investing in them, you are not revealing a single thing to the world at large. While banks and brokerages require the extensive disclosure of client information to governmental agencies, private gold coins are absolutely free from this kind of intrusiveness.

As a rule of thumb, if you are trading in and out of gold several times a year, bullion might be a better asset for that strategy. Yet private coins are geared to the saver/investor who wants wealth preservation over a longer time-frame and when privacy and a lack of government interference is important.

In short, buying private gold & silver coins offers you numerous benefits over gold bullion:

- Private gold & silver coins can have an expanding premium to their melt value and often outperform bullion investments based on their increasing rarity and demand
- Private gold & silver coins can be less volatile that bullion because there is no ETF or paper-traded market determining their value; rather, their value is affected more by true physical demand than bullion investments
- Private gold coins come from the days of "mind your own business" and can be bought and sold without any formal paperwork
- Private gold coins are a great way to safely store wealth outside the banking system and prevent government access to it.

Deadly Myth #6: All Gold Can Be Recalled During Crises

During the darkest days of the Great Depression in 1933, President Franklin D. Roosevelt was desperate to stabilize the U.S. dollar from the ravages of a shrinking economy. By executive order, Roosevelt recalled U.S. gold coins from U.S. citizens in exchange for paper currency notes, under the severe penalty of a $10,000 fine and a maximum 10-year imprisonment for anyone who failed to cooperate. Some historians believe this was the beginning of the "shrinking U.S. Dollar," as the government melted the majority of confiscated coins into bars and then devalued the dollar, raising gold's value by nearly 75%.

Today, some investors are weary of buying physical gold because they remember the recall of 1933 and fear the government may recall gold again during bad economic times. But they fail to realize that, while not all gold is subject to recall, more importantly the incentive to take gold from private citizens no longer exists since we are no longer on a gold standard. In 1933, every solvent citizen of the country had some physical gold and silver. (Today, physical gold only makes up less than 1% of the assets in the average American retirement account or investment portfolio). As a form of government stimulus intended to get the country out of the Depression and create some economic growth, the government needed to recall all the nation's gold and begin their course of dollar devaluation via fiat currencies and debt accumulation.

Roosevelt's 1933 executive order excluded coins that had rare or historic relevance or value above they're melt value. This exclusion still stands today, meaning that pre-1933 coins – those that escaped the first recall – as well as coins that are minted in limited quantities or are semi-numismatic, are still private and exempt from government recall. But again, the government has no incentive to recall an asset that very few of its citizens have possession of. The beauty of the modern financial system to a government or its banking factions is that all the wealth in the system can be accessed at any time with a keystroke on a computer. If you believe, like many do, that our government will at some point confiscate its citizens' wealth, you are smart to move some of your wealth into physical gold because that removes some of your wealth from the one place where the government has the easiest access to it: the modern banking system.

Deadly Myth #7: Gold Is for Collectors, Not Investors

A number of our clients at Wholesale Direct Metals initially make the mistake of referring to gold & silver coins as "collector" coins. While it's true that many people do collect gold & silver coins as a hobby, it is severely limiting to think of gold & silver coins just in terms of their value to "collectors." We call private coins "investment-grade" coins because they are as durable, well-performing and wealth-protecting as any investment products on the market. And the fact that they are also valuable to collectors means that they are scarce and maintain an intrinsic premium value over gold bullion, all of which make private coins a great investment for anyone looking to grow their money and protect their wealth.

THE 7 EMPOWERING SIGNS
NOW IS THE RIGHT TIME TO INVEST IN GOLD

Now that we've dispelled the deadly myths that often prevent people from making prudent investments in gold, you still might wonder when is the right time to invest in gold. Any smart investor wants to be able to read the tea leaves and know what signs indicate a good time to buy. So in the next section, we examine "The 7 Empowering Signs That Now Is the Right Time to Invest in Gold."

Empowering Sign #1: The Dollar is Falling

We all know the damage caused by the devaluation of the U.S. dollar. Every day, your money is worth less than it was yesterday. Your purchasing power shrinks and your investment portfolio suffers. The good news is, with each downtick of the U.S. dollar comes an uptick in the value of gold. Fundamentally, gold's value increases because the amount of printed fiat currency is also increasing. Simply put, the increase of fiat currency devalues fiat currency. As long as the Federal Reserve and the central banks around the world keep printing fiat currency, the price of gold will continue to rise.

Investing in gold can form the cornerstone of a conservative or aggressive portfolio because it tends to move in the opposite direction of paper investments and the U.S. Dollar. It has become even more popular as a necessary addition to any diversified portfolio in the last few years. You buy gold to hedge the items of perceived performance in your portfolio, but don't be surprised if gold continues to outperform most everything else if we keep printing currency, accumulating debt, and spending money we don't have.

Protecting yourself from U.S. dollar devaluation and currency debasement is an important aspect of preserving your wealth. Yet, protection from a falling U.S. dollar can also be tricky in the current economic environment. Let's look at how and why. In the past, before the game of global "competitive currency destruction" began, one could have bought a competing currency or other country's currency, which should have become more valuable as the dollar deflated and served as a hedge to a falling U.S. dollar. The problem with that strategy now is that all the central banks around the world are printing fiat currency in order to be able to trade with one another. The fact that all fiat currencies are all being debased is an effect of the global effort to kick-the-can and avoid painful default and or restructuring, which means there is no longer any security in foreign currencies.

Holding any asset that trades globally in terms of U.S. dollars should serve the purpose of hedging a falling dollar. Unfortunately, this isn't going to work for you. You're not going to store barrels of oil in the garage. Demand for something like diamonds is far too volatile to call anything about it "protection." And real estate brings tax issues, loan issues (bank involvement) and maintenance fees, not to mention real estate isn't going anywhere until unemployment and wage growth get better. So gold makes the most sense as a wealth preserver. This should make perfect sense, since that is exactly what gold is designed to be and ultimately what it is. Not only does gold protect you against a falling U.S. dollar, it protects you from the monetization and debasement of all fiat currencies and paper promises.

And even in a default scenario, it protects you because gold loves chaos, debt and a falling U.S. Dollar.

Empowering Sign #2: The Debt is Rising

Many economists have argued that going into debt is sometimes a necessary and unavoidable way to maintain our nation's infrastructure, protect our national interests, and keep the economy stable. Yet we all know there's a serious price to pay when the national debt skyrockets and remains at unmanageable levels for decades. The value of our currency shrinks, meaning your money in the bank and many of your investments are shrinking in value right along with it. So, how do you protect your investments against the scourge of national debt?

History shows us that the most reliable hedge against rising national debts is investing in gold. Just take a look at the last few years as an example. In 2008, the national debt stood at $9 trillion and the price of gold was $850 per ounce. In less than 2 years, the national debt rose 67% to $15 trillion. Meanwhile, gold rose at exactly the same rate: 67% to $1425 per ounce. Now, you may agree or disagree with why the debt was increased, yet we can all agree that the national debt has increased precipitously over the last decade, and gold has once again proven to be the most reliable hedge against rising debts.

Empowering Sign #3: The Fed Keeps Printing Money

We've already examined how printing money and increasing the national debt devalues our currency and spawns a proportionate increase in the price of gold. What must be emphasized is that the actions of our Federal Reserve and policy makers is not something in the past; the fact is, the Fed continues to print money as we speak.

Presently, the U.S. prints money to buy treasuries to keep rates low. Not only does this cause a major drop in the value of the U.S. Dollar, it also makes it impossible for our trading partners to sell us anything. So they all turn on their own printing presses to "equalize" the value of global currencies by devaluing their own currencies against the dollar. Needless to say, this current central bank action makes holding any fiat currency a huge risk and almost a guarantee to lose your purchasing power and wealth. So as the Fed keeps printing money, it becomes more and more imperative to own gold as a hedge against plummeting global currencies.

Empowering Sign #4: The Stock Market Is Losing Value Even As It Rises

To understand how the stock market actually loses value even as it rises, you need to go back to the crisis that has been created by increasing debt and printing money. As an illustration, use your imagination and pretend the U.S. government, Europe and the central banks of the world act like a public company. This company has 100 shares at $1 dollar per share. To pay down its debt and make the debt more manageable, the company prints more shares. The only way to keep the company afloat is to pay interest payments, so the company prints even more shares. But the stockholders aren't made aware; they think their shares are still worth $1 dollar, yet the company has sold 100,000 more shares and used the money to pay down debts. This is essentially what the Federal Reserve is doing with the U.S. currency. And in response, the international community uses U.S. dollars to buy gold, silver, sugar, cotton, oil, and other commodities. Why? Because even when the stock market goes up to Dow 15,000, in real dollars that's closer to Dow 9,000.

The example that is often cited is the devastating two-year inflation rate of 24.7 percent from 1979-1980, the highest in modern-day America. During the five worst years of inflation in U.S. history, the average return on Dow stocks was significantly lower than the rate of inflation. Not the most inspiring reason for investing wholly in stocks. Meanwhile, gold reacted protectively by hitting $850 an ounce and silver reached $55. This is fundamentally why private gold and silver coins have a history of being complementary to traditional stocks, meaning they actually tend to move in the opposite direction of stocks.

So clearly, private gold and silver coins maintain an important position in a prudent portfolio. And not just as an antidote for inflation, high interest rates, or political uncertainty. Although perfectly suited for these roles, investment-grade private coins are best evaluated on their own record of long-term growth. Converting your assets from cash, money markets and mutual funds into physical U.S. gold provides you with protection and diversification against the shrinking dollar, inflation and volatile global stock markets.

Empowering Sign #5: The Wealthiest People in the World Are Buying Gold

It's often said that, if you want to become wealthy, just look at what wealthy people do and follow suit. And if you're already wealthy and want to stay that way, pay close attention to how the wealthy class maintains their wealth over many generations. What's the common denominator in both cases? Investment in gold.

You need not look much further than the top .001% -- central bankers who essentially control the world and most of its wealth – to see how they protect themselves from the debasement of the U.S. dollar (and global fiat currencies), and copy what they do to your own personal advantage. After all, the central banks know when they are going to print money, and gold becomes the true currency of central bankers. Central banks have been net buyers of gold for nearly a decade now, and countries like India, China, Brazil, Korea and many others have been buying literally tons of gold at a time. So be your own central banker, so to speak. Protect yourself from the debasement of currency by investing in gold.

Empowering Sign #6: Retail Investors Are Just Now Discovering Gold

When we countered the "gold boom is over" myth, we mentioned that penetration and participation in gold investing was far from being on a mass scale. In fact, even when gold peaked at $870 in 1980, gold made up just 5% of the average investment portfolio. Today, even with the precipitous rise in gold, exposure to gold makes up less than 1.5% of the wealth in the U.S.. Shockingly, wealth today is still concentrated in paper.

What this all means is that retail investors – average people looking to grow their money or protect their investments – are just now waking up to gold. This is exactly why the majority of experts who are bullish on gold point to the fact that retail investment in gold is just beginning. Since gold tends to move in the opposite direction of paper investments and the U.S. dollar, gold is soon to become even more popular as a necessary addition to any diversified portfolio. Federal bailout programs and stimulus measures have caused a major increase in the volume of dollars printed and have also caused the federal budget deficit to grow to historical and unprecedented levels. As a result, investing in gold and holding hard gold as a hedge has become more important for Americans than ever before. And it's only the beginning.

Empowering Sign #7: Gold Has Been a Durable Investment for 5,000 Years

How can you argue with an investment that has been a top performer for over 5,000 years? Indeed, gold has outlasted every single debt-based paper currency that human beings have ever invented. As the Roman Empire crumbled around them, Roman emperors sought refuge in their asset of last resort: gold. Gold hording during the final days of the Roman Empire crippled the global economy, leaving only those who owned gold any real security from the collapsing empire.

For over 5,000 years, gold has been the purest form of money and the oldest, most durable wealth-preserving asset on the planet. Governments can't devalue it. It has no debts, no board of directors, no politicians or central bankers who can manipulate its value. That's why investing in gold has survived every economy in history, has outlasted every paper currency ever printed, and has preserved investors' purchasing power over a span of over 5,000 years. Negative economic, political, environmental, or monetary policy conditions contribute to a rising gold price. This is the reason gold has always been referred to as a perfect diversifier.

THE BEST GOLD & SILVER INVESTMENTS

When the DOW moved past 18,000 in late 2014, financial managers everywhere were very quick to declare victory for stocks. Gold bullion had its worst year in decades, mainly because of paper-gold manipulation and soaring stocks. The CNBC crowd were too busy patting each other on the backs to report the fact that stocks had been artificially propped up by several years of reckless Fed money-printing that everyone knew would have to end sooner or later. So as the DOW raged on and bullion took a beating, everyone in the mainstream media seemed to forget about a certain investment that has tripled the DOW and nearly doubled bullion for the last 40 years!

The Private Gold & Silver Coin Market

People who know how to think for themselves (and refuse to listen to self-serving money managers or CNBC talking heads) have long understood the benefits of investing long-term in physical gold & silver and limiting their exposure to paper-based assets like stocks. However, for the last 40+ years, the smart money in gold & silver investing hasn't been going to bullion, and it certainly isn't going to paper gold in the form of the Gold ETF. The smart money in gold & silver investing has been going straight to "private" coins, to the tune of a 6200% return on investment since 1970!

Private coins are non-recallable & non-reportable and include such coins as the Arctic Fox gold & silver, the $20 St. Gaudens gold, Liberty Head gold, Indian Head gold, European fractionals, gold proofs from the U.S. Mint, peace silver dollars, Morgan silver dollars, 90% "junk silver," and silver proofs. Why are these coins referred to as "private"? Because by law, they have much less visibility to the powers-that-be when you buy and sell them. They are one of the last private investments from the days of "mind your own business," and their performance over the last 40+ years is undeniable. For these reasons, millions of people have joined the private gold & silver coin market to protect their savings & retirement against government and corporate corruption.

Private Coins vs. the DOW & Bullion

For better or (mostly) worse, the DOW has been the standard against which all investments have been compared for nearly a century. Financial analysts consider any investment that outperforms the DOW over an extended period of time to be a solid investment. So, how have private coins fared vs. the DOW? The numbers are off the charts (see graph on next page):

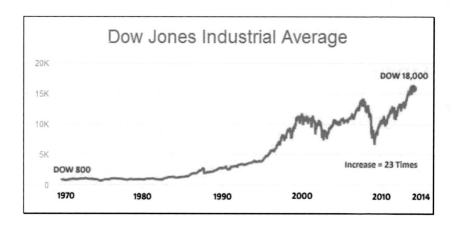

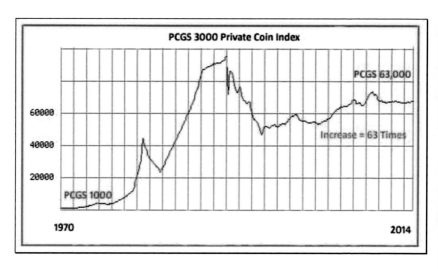

So while the DOW rose a respectable 23 times from 1970 to 2014, private coins rose a staggering 63 times during the same time period! Keep in mind that some economic indicators show inflation of about 15 times since 1970, so the DOW barely stays ahead of inflation.

So, how do private coins compare to bullion? The numbers are almost as staggering:

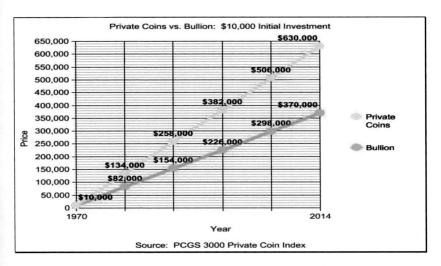

Private Coins vs. Bullion: $10,000 Initial Investment

Source: PCGS 3000 Private Coin Index

That's a return of 63 times for private coins vs. a return of 37 times for bullion! So an investment of $10,000 in private coins in 1970 would have netted you $630,000 by 2014! As you can see, while bullion significantly outperforms the DOW, private coins significantly outperform both the DOW and bullion. And keep this in mind when comparing bullion & private coins to the DOW: these charts are taken AFTER a year in which the DOW hit record levels and the price of bullion had tanked. So even after a year in which stocks skyrocketed and bullion fell, both private coins and bullion still significantly out-perform the DOW over the long-term!

Safe, Secure & Low Volatility

Typically, an investment that enjoys huge returns also brings with it high volatility and huge downside risk. But the amazing thing about private coins is that, despite their huge returns, they are actually quite steady and have much less volatility than stocks or bullion. As an illustration, just compare private coins to bullion in 2013, when bullion had its worst year in decades:

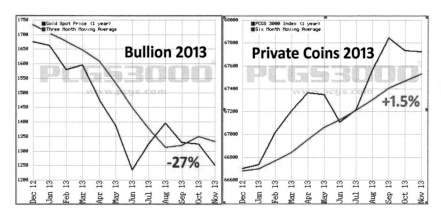

While bullion fell 27% for the year, private coins actually INCREASED 1.5%. So even during tough times, private coins have proven to be one of the safest, most stable investments in the marketplace.

A recent study, which was originally done for the Joint Committee on Taxation of the House and Senate, showed that U.S. private coins were a better hedge than bullion and produced better investment returns. This study served as the basis for Congressional legislation that provided for the inclusion of gold in Individual Retirement Accounts. The conclusions over the 28-year period were outstanding:

- Private coins were a better inflation hedge than bullion.

- Private coins were a better hedge than bullion against falling prices for stocks and bonds.

- Private coins produced significant profits even during periods when the price of bullion was falling.

- The average annual return on private coins was more than 200% greater than the return on bullion.

- The return on private coins in their best year was approximately 100% greater than the return on bullion in its best year.

- The return on private coins in their best three years was approximately 100% greater than the return on bullion was in its best three years.

Join the Private Gold & Silver Coin Market

So in short, private coins are non-reportable, non-recallable, have tripled the DOW and nearly doubled bullion, and are often much more stable and less volatile than stocks or bullion. What's more, some private coins are even eligible to be placed in an IRA. So if you're one of the millions of people looking to diversify and protect your savings & retirement with hard physical assets, it's time to join the private gold & silver coin market.

SECURE YOUR RETIREMENT WITH A GOLD IRA

If you're like most investors, you're worried about jeopardizing your retirement in risky stocks and bonds. If you'd like a safe and time-proven retirement portfolio that has a long history of steady growth, then you'd be wise to secure your IRA or 401K with gold.

Opening a Gold IRA offers you many advantages over other IRAs:

- Owning a Gold IRA means you actually own gold
- Gold IRA's can include any combination of gold, silver, platinum, or palladium
- Gold never becomes worthless like some stocks and bonds
- Gold has a proven history of steady growth
- Gold is a tangible asset with far less risk than other investment assets

Securing your IRA or 401K with gold is actually a very simple process:

- Start a new IRA backed by Gold
- Transfer your existing IRA into a Gold IRA
- Transfer funds from a previous employer's 401K into a Gold IRA

So in short, Gold IRAs offer you all the advantages of investing in gold with the many advantages of securing your money in an IRA.

CONCLUSION: WAITING IS THE HARDEST PART

Even with all the convincing evidence that now is the right time to invest in gold, it's understandable that you might need a little more time to buy gold. People need to convert their green paper money and their debt-based savings into gold when it's comfortable for them to do it. It's important to note, however, that most investors who have waited to buy gold over the past 10 years have cost themselves a lot of money. Remember, you don't buy physical gold today to sell it next week, so "market timing" is less important. The dollar's decay has been a long road in one direction; and yes, there have been short bursts of dollar strength (and thus gold weakness) along the way. But waiting to own gold is the same as waiting for the dollar to fall.

Let's be crystal clear about the concept of "waiting" in this type of global monetary landscape. If you are considering gold, you must be aware of the following issues: the volatility of banking systems around the world, unsustainable national debts globally, the decay of fiat money, and the general frustration with our taxation systems, trade systems and Wall Street's basic functions. After the meltdown of large institutions like Lehman Brothers and MF Global, anyone "waiting" to protect their financial wealth is simply walking on thin ice while juggling fire. You either get it, or you don't. And those that get it... aren't waiting. That's not to say you don't still have some very good questions about investing in gold and silver. That's why we continually address investor concerns on our website, and you are always welcome to contact me directly with any of your questions or concerns. Just visit www.WholesaleDirectMetals.com.

About the Author

Damon Geller

Damon Geller serves as CEO of Wholesale Direct Metals and is one of the most respected gold and hard asset managers in the industry. His trend analysis is widely read and quoted, and he is often invited to appear on financial radio and television programs nationwide. Damon's insights are carefully derived from Fed and monetary policy, debt-based economies and the history of money. This background supports his exceptional ability to interpret how current policy frameworks affect numerous investments. Damon doesn't reserve his expertise and trend forecasting for high net-worth clients only; rather he freely shares his views and knowledge with anyone seriously interested in investing in gold and other precious metals. Damon's company, Wholesale Direct Metals, has received the highest marks in client services, delivery time, investment returns and customer service. Damon received an economics degree from The University of California-San Diego. Damon's feature analysis, "Ask the Expert," can be read on his company website:

www.WholesaleDirectMetals.com

19053708R00052

Made in the USA
Middletown, DE
02 April 2015